Harrow

in old picture postcards

including Harrow, Wealdstone, Kenton, Stanmore, Hatch End, Pinner, North Harrow, Rayners Lane and South Harrow

by
Dennis F. Edwards

European Library - Zaltbommel/Netherlands MCMLXXXV

GB   ISBN 90 288 3192 4 / CIP

European Library in Zaltbommel/Netherlands publishes among other things the following series:

IN OLD PICTURE POSTCARDS *is a series of books which sets out to show what a particular place looked like and what life was like in Victorian and Edwardian times. A book about virtually every town in the United Kingdom is to be published in this series. By the end of this year about 175 different volumes will have appeared. 1,250 books have already been published devoted to the Netherlands with the title* **In oude ansichten.** *In Germany, Austria and Switzerland 500, 60 and 15 books have been published as* **In alten Ansichten;** *in France by the name* **En cartes postales anciennes** *and in Belgium as* **En cartes postales anciennes** *and/or* **In oude prentkaarten** *150 respectively 400 volumes have been published.*

For further particulars about published or forthcoming books, apply to your bookseller or direct to the publisher.

This edition has been printed and bound by Grafisch Bedrijf De Steigerpoort in Zaltbommel/Netherlands.

INTRODUCTION

Harrow is world famous for its school, and its church spire, which rises above a green mantle of trees on Harrow Hill. Until the early years of this century, Harrow Hill stood like an island amid a sea of green fields that spread away to the wooded slopes of Harrow Weald and Stanmore on the north, and the lush, elm lined meadows of the Pinner country to the west. The nearest suburbs of London were then almost 8 miles away.

The coming of the local railways changed all that. Today most of that countryside has been replaced by thousands of houses and small gardens, shops, factories and roads. Harrow Hill alone stands unspoiled, with a few fields around its base, amid the red roofs of suburban London.

Although one of the earliest railways (the London and Birmingham, 1837) passed near Harrow Hill, it had little effect at first. Then towards the end of the nineteenth century, industry began to appear near the line. Kodak Limited set up a factory in 1891 at Wealdstone, followed by Hamilton Brushes in 1898 and Winsor and Newton (artists materials) in 1897. The result was that Wealdstone began to grow — from 211 houses 1881 to 3,500 by the end of 1911.

But it was the opening of the Metropolitan Railway in 1880, with its station at the foot of the Hill, that began the transformation of the area from rural township to suburbia. Houses spread quickly over the market gardens and fields of Greenhill, to link Harrow with Wealdstone by 1914.

In the years between 1919 and 1939, there was a great explosion of building. The fast and frequent electric train services brought home seekers out to Harrow and other local villages in their thousands. For this was the age of 'Metro-land', when a new semi-detached house, with a stained glass window in the hall, a hot water boiler in the kitchen and a tiled bathroom, was every young housewife's dream. The new houses could be bought for £650 by paying £5 deposit and 75p a week!

The old Harrow hamlets and villages of Hooking Green, Roxeth, Greenhill, Kenton, Pinner and Stanmore were soon merged into a 'Greater Harrow' of endless streets, parks and shopping parades. Artists have been recording Harrow for at least 300 years, but it was the crowds of day trippers, walkers and cyclists who came to see Harrow Hill, Pinner and the woods of Harrow Weald in Edwardian days, who created a market for picture postcards.

Local photographers such as Coles of Watford and F.C. Hebblewhite of Wealdstone, were soon hard at work photographing the area. One of Hebblewhite's advertisements of 1912 for his High Street shop says *Noted throughout the district... 250 views to select from... all from 1d each.* Other local postcards were simply marked *published by...* with the name of a local stationer's shop, such as Wenham of Wealdstone. There were also cards by Valentine and other well-known national postcard publishers.

Harrow in old picture postcards includes not only Harrow-on-the-Hill, but the villages that today have grown up to make the London Borough of Harrow. The cards span the years from the turn of the century to the middle 1930's.

Many of the views show you a Harrow that is now unrecognizable. A Harrow of quiet places, of many trees and hedges; large houses and muddy country lanes; ponds where cattle drank; picturesques public houses and old, charming yet insanitary cottages.

Harrow was a district, which a railway guide book described in 1912 as being... *where the din and turmoil of the streets are exchanged for an aspect of spreading landscapes, of trees and green fields, where no sound assails the ears saving the singing of the birds.*

Publicity such as this was so effective that thousands of Londoners came to make their homes in the Harrow area, transforming it in less than a generation into a busy London suburb.

HARROW

1. Victorian photograph of the old water pump at the junction of High Street and West
Street. Pails of water were sold here for ½d. The pump and its canopy were replaced with
a marble drinking fountain in 1880.

2. The King's Head Hotel and the Green about 1902. The inn dates back to 1535, although the present buildings are mostly nineteenth century. From 1824 the London coach left from outside. The buildings on the far left were the premises of the London and County Bank. Later the Harrow Council had their offices next door. Across the road was Harrow's first public hall, later converted to a cinema called the 'Elite'.

3. Looking down Church Hill to The Headmaster's House about eighty years ago. The building dates from 1838, when it replaced an earlier house destroyed by fire. The buildings on the right of this picture, which included The Crown and Anchor inn, were swept away when the War Memorial Building and ornamental steps were built after the First World War.

Harrow on the Hill, High Street.

4. High Street at the junction of West Street about 1910. On the left is the old post office whilst across the street are The Headmasters House, The Old House (it was the New King's Head inn between 1720 and 1800), and Flambards.

High Street, Harrow

5. High Street in Edwardian days, with the office of the 'Harrow Gazette' on the left. The newspaper was founded by William Winkley in 1855.

6. A slightly later view of High Street. Wright Cooper, the baker, opened his first shop here. He learned his skills as a chef with P & O and his Harrow business was so successful that he opened a second shop in Station Road 1900 — a café and restaurant that flourished until about 25 years ago.

Old Schools, Harrow

Valentines Series

7. Old Schools Building of 1615, with later additions. The school was founded by John Lyon in 1592. On the right are the buildings later demolished for the War Memorial Building in the early 1920's.

HARROW SCHOOL, 220. (GOING TO CHAPEL.)

8. Pre-1914 scene, with the Old Schools (left). In the distance is the Speech Room of 1877. The Harrow boys are proceeding to Chapel, some dressed in army cadet uniforms. During the First World War that was soon to follow, many ex-Harrovians lost their lives and they are remembered in the War Memorial Building which was to rise in the place of the houses in the middle of this view.

9. Church Hill about 1910 (left) with the lych gate to St. Mary's Church at the top. The gate was erected in memory of the Reverend John Cunningham (1811-1861). When Harrow School began to worship in its own chapel in 1868, Cunningham feared that the boys would be led to 'Popery'!

Sudbury Road

Stengel & Co. Dresden-Berlin. 14431

Dec 11.ᵗʰ 1903

HARROW
ON THE HILL

Only to say we
are well & hope
to answer your
nice long letter
next week.
Margaret is here
she saw Milly
a few days ago &
thought she was
looking very ill
I have between
80 & 100 letters or
cards to send off
besides the many
family ones which
B. writes
Her best love to you all
M L S

10. Sudbury Road, at the junction with Roxeth Hill. The water cart is taking supplies
from a wayside stand pipe. Water carts performed a valuable service in summer, keeping
the dust from the local roads.

Sudbury Road, Harrow.

11. Looking up Sudbury Hill towards the centre of Harrow about 1913. The large houses seen here are typical of the many erected for school officials and wealthy London businessmen during the later half of the nineteenth century.

Harrow, Grove Hill

12. Grove Hill was the scene of Britain's first car accident on 25th February 1899. A Daimler Waggonette, with a test driver and passengers, came down at high speed, and when turning the corner by the signpost, one of the rear wheels collapsed. The driver, Edwin Sewell, was killed and another person died in hospital later.

HARROW ON THE HILL, WAR MEMORIAL

13. Grove Hill in the 1920's. The houses were the homes of many famous people. Before Peterborough Hill was built, Grove Hill was the main road linking the Hill with Harrow Weald.

14. Steam train arriving at Harrow-on-the-Hill from Uxbridge 1904. This was in the short period of steam operation before electric trains began on 1st January 1905. The original Metropolitan station at Harrow opened on 2nd August 1880 and was constructed in a style that was 'in keeping with the dignity and associations of Harrow Hill'. The station was enlarged in 1908 and completely rebuilt in 1939.

15. By electric express to Baker Street 1908. One of the new 'steeple back' type electric locomotives with a train of steam carriages from Aylesbury, passing Sheepcote Road Bridge. The change over point for steam/electric locomotives on Metropolitan Aylesbury trains was at Harrow-on-the-Hill from 1908 to 1924.

Wealdstone.

18-5-03

Station Road.

Can you spare just a few minutes to let me know how you are keeping have been thinking so much of you lately

The Wrench Series, No. 2773

16. Station Road near 'Poet's Corner' and the Wealdstone station bridge, 1903. Bridge Street Schools are on the left. They were demolished for the Civic Centre in the early 1970's. But the houses on the right survive. The quiet road has now become a busy through route.

Greenhill Parade, Harrow

17. Station Road and St. Anne's Road, Greenhill. Greenhill grew rapidly after the opening of the Metropolitan Railway and eventually even the front gardens of the villas seen here were built on with shops. Just beyond the parade of shops stood The White House, replaced by William Soper's drapery store about 1914. It was eventually to grow into the town's main department store. Now rebuilt, it is a branch of Debenham's.

HARROW. STATION ROAD

74652

18. The twin domes of The Coliseum were a well-known landmark in Station Road for nearly forty years. Harrow's first luxury cinema, The Coliseum, had plush seats, and an American soda fountain. The local M.P., Oswald Mosley, performed the opening ceremony on Monday 11th October 1920. In July 1939, the building became a theatre and through the war years and after became a popular centre for classical music, shows and plays.

HARROW, COLLEGE ROAD

78209

19. A later 1930's view of College Road. Modern shops have replaced most of the villas. An ST type bus (probably on route 140) trundles towards Station Road and the tower of the Baptist Church. The building was another well-known feature of central Harrow from 1908 to 1983.

HIGH STREET, WEALDSTONE.

WEALDSTONE
20. Wealdstone began to expand following the arrival of local industry. One of the first firms was Kodak (1891). The High Street began to grow, with rows of shops to serve the new population. Wenham's stationery shop and library was a popular place to buy post-cards.

21. Extension work in progress at the Kodak factory about eighty years ago. George Eastman, the company's founder, chose 7 acres of open farmland on the outskirts of Wealdstone and built his first photographic factory in Europe in 1890. The clean air and freedom from city dust were no doubt important factors for the manufacture of photographic plates and films. One of the buildings bears the famous Kodak slogan: *You press the button. We do the rest.*

22. The corner of Mason's Avenue and High Street about 1904, with F.E. Bunting's cycle shop. Mr. Bunting, a former booking clerk at Wealdstone station, had just decided to cater for the latest passing craze — motoring. In the distance can be seen Arthur Flint's drapery store, where the annual sale offered all goods for under 1/- (5p).

23. Byron Recreation Ground at the end of Peel Road was opened in 1899. In 1911 it was the scene of the local celebration for the Coronation of George V. A wooden structure called 'Coronation Villa' was built and formed part of the great fireworks-display. No doubt Mr. Taylor, the park superintendent, who lived in the house seen here, kept a watchful eye over the proceedings.

Blackberry Lane Woodstone

24. Blackberry Lane (now Church Lane) was a favourite place for blackberrying. Gray's Fair was held in the adjacent fields. Much of the land was owned by New College, Oxford, who sold it all for building in the 1920's.

HARROW WEALD LANE, WEALDSTONE

This is my way to the station. —

25. The year is 1880 and a Governess poses with her small 'charges' outside one of the new villas in the rapidly growing suburb of Wealdstone.

BELMOUNT, WEALDSTONE.

26. The path across Stanmore Golf Course from Belmont. The name Belmont was derived from 'Bell Mount' – the hill that rises up from the flat fields of Kenton.

27. Headstone Manor is the oldest secular building in Harrow. First mentioned in the ninth century, it was for centuries owned by the Archbishops of Canterbury. There is a local legend that Thomas à Becket spent his last Christmas here. This 1906 picture shows the moat that still surrounds the house — a favourite spot for boating and fishing in those days.

THE POND AND LANE, HARROW WEALD, WEALDSTONE.

28. Anthony's or Weald Farm, was situated opposite The Red Lion. The farm was a childhood home of novelist Anthony Trollope. For many years it was farmed by Bill and Tom Durrant. Then by J.S. Anthony, who ran a large dairy business. You can see one of his carts, with the horse taking a drink from the pond at the junction of Weald Lane.

KENTON

29. The Rest Hotel was a favourite place for cyclists and walkers. *Kenton is a dreamy hamlet set in a sea of emerald, with a few cottages* said a guide book of 1920. Ten years later Kenton was already developing into a suburb. The Rest Hotel was rebuilt as a large public house and parades of shops were built along Kenton Road.

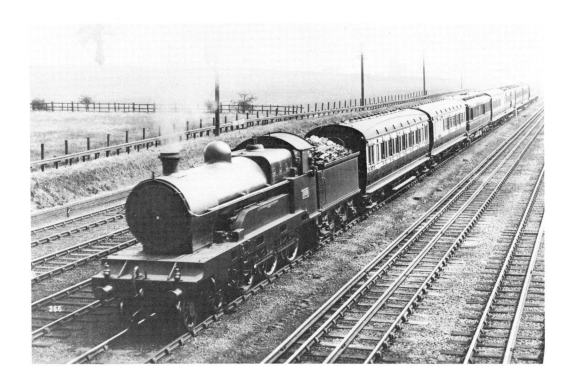

30. A LMS express near Kenton in the 1920's. In the foreground are the suburban tracks laid down from Euston to Watford in the 1900's. They were electrified for the extension of the Bakerloo tube in 1917.

31. Liverpool to Wembley excursion train passing Kenton on the way to the British Empire Exhibition, 1924. The bridge carrying the Metropolitan and LNER lines is in the background. The open fields to the right were soon to be covered in houses.

32. Although a few houses appeared at Kenton before 1914, large scale developments only began in the late 1920's. Edwards were the agents for HRP Estates, who built on land in Kenton Lane formerly owned by St. Bartholomew's Hospital, London.

33. Artistic homes for businessmen 1927-style. The Northwick Park Estate was built on land once owned by the Churchill family, Lords of the Manor of Harrow. Their country seat was at Northwick Park near Batsford, in the Cotswolds. Northwick Park Station at Kenton was opened in 1923 to serve the new suburb.

STANMORE

34. On Stanmore Hill before the First World War, with London General Omnibus Company bus on route 142. This country service was popular with Londoners seeking a breath of fresh air and perhaps a pint of beer at one of the Stanmore inns.

35. Ginger's Butcher's shop 1890. The delivery cart is ready to take the orders of meat to the large houses hidden away in the woods of the Stanmore hills. Nobody seemed to mind that the joints of meat must have got a good coating of dust and flies from the road!

36. So little traffic disturbed the tranquility of Stanmore Hill 85 years ago, that a customer at the village store could leave his cart and horse parked at right angles to the kerb. It is interesting to compare the smart buildings with the same spot in the next picture, taken 25 years later.

37. Stanmore was growing fast by 1935 and it was no longer fashionable to shop in Stanmore Hill. The ST-type bus is on route 142 to Kilburn. At the Abercorn Arms (named after the eighteenth century owners of Bentley Priory), lunch is advertised at 2/6 (13p) and dinner at 3/6 (16p), but few passengers on the bus could afford such luxury.

38. The original Stanmore station, which opened on 18th December 1890. It was the terminus of a branch from Wealdstone and was built by Frederick Gordon, who had converted Bentley Priory into a country hotel. The line was closed between Belmont and Stanmore in 1953.

39. Stanmore Broadway 1931 and a local shop keeper stares at the photographer from the Metropolitan Railway publicity office, who has come to record the village for a guide book. The Metropolitan Railway from Wembley Park to Stanmore opened in 1932.

HATCH END

40. The Royal Commercial Travellers Schools were opened beside the LNWR main line in 1855. The original foundation was for 140 pupils, but the school was enlarged in 1866 for the accommodation of 300. Further extensions were made in 1905, when a new school building costing £20,000 was erected. Most of the buildings were cleared away in the 1970's.

Photograph by M. L. EMERY.

S. Anselm's, Hatch End, Pinner.

PINNER.

41. St. Anselm's Church by F.E. Jones was consecrated in 1895 to serve the growing number of houses near the LNWR station. It replaced a temporary Chapel of Ease called All Souls.

S 9084   ROYSTON PARK, ROAD, PINNER.

42. Improved railway services and the rebuilding of Hatch End Station by C. Horsley in 1911, helped to develop Hatch End. Royston Park and the adjacent The Avenue were typical of the early 1900's development.

PINNER

43. High Street a century ago, with The Crown Inn (demolished 1898) on the far left. The figure just beyond is possibly W.F. Petley, owner of the grocery shop, which later became a branch of W.H. Cullen. The tall buildings opposite (erected by Daniel Gurney a few years before) were so ugly that local people named them 'The Barracks'.

44. This view of High Street dates from the early years of the present century. 'The Barracks' on the right have been converted into shops. Further along was the Lamb Inn and at one period, the post office.

PINNER.

45. The postcard was one of a series issued towards the end of last century by a magazine called 'Idle Moments' 'Obtainable all newsagents 1d'. The Queens Head on the left, was first mentioned in 1705, and was the departure point for the London coach.

46. Pinner Fair has been held in High Street and Bridge Street every year since 1336. This is an 1885 view, with J. Pettigrew's famous steam driven 'Great London Roundabout'. Pettigrew is sitting by the booth in the centre of this picture, near the Roundabout. He was well-known in the show business.

"Ye Cocoa Tree," Pinner

47. Ye Cocoa Tree was a favourite rendez-vous for day trippers to Pinner. Originally a private house called 'Belle Vue', it was converted into a café by a strong supporter of the Temperance Movement, William Barber. The establishment had an 'inn' sign depicting a tree with steaming cups of cocoa instead of fruit! The building became the Conservative Club in 1931 and in recent years, business premises.

PINNER CHURCH AND YE COCOA TREE.

Coles, Photographer, Watford.

48. The people standing at the top of High Street are waiting to go in to the Cocoa Tree (left) for one of the restaurant's celebrated strawberry teas. The small shop on the right was a butchers, with convenient slaughter house attached, ensuring that the meat was fresh — essential in the days before refrigeration.

Pinner Church

49. St. John's parish church from Church Lane 1905. The tall, ivy covered monument is to William Loudon and was erected by his son John, the early nineteenth century horticulturalist, in 1809. Its design incorporated a stone 'coffin', which gave rise to the legend that William was 'buried in air'!

HIGH STREET, SHOWING WAR MEMORIAL PINNER

50. Looking down High Street from the church in 1929. The old cottages on the far left, behind the War Memorial, were replaced in 1931 by Grange Court, a block of 'Tudor' style flats and shops.

Cook Memorial Fountain, Pinner

51. Nower Hill and the Green 1904. Nearby was Nower House (demolished 1964), the home of the Heal family, who owned the department store in London's Tottenham Court Road.

NOWER HILL, PINNER.

Downer. Photo.

52. Another view of Nower Hill, with Tooke's Fountain, erected by public subscription in 1886 to commemorate William Arthur Tooke, a famous local benefactor.

53. Chapel Lane railway bridge 1914. The shop on the corner was owned for many years by the Ellement family. The Methodists used to meet in the last cottage on the right. The only surviving building in this picture today is the cottage on the far left.

PINNER — MARLBOROUGH HILL.

54. Bridge Street looking down to the main part of the village. The postcard is wrongly captioned 'Marlborough Hill'. The timbered building on the right is Dear's Farm. It was replaced by the Langham Cinema in 1935. To many new residents of Pinner at the time it seemed like a giant step forward for modern progress!

55. Love Lane ánd the old fire station. Under the trees, the horse bus driven by George Bridge is making yet another trip to Hatch End station. The bus service ran from 1886 until 1914.

CECIL PARK, PINNER

56. Metropolitan Railway Surplus Lands Committee's Cecil Park Estate next to Pinner station. It was one of the very first housing ventures of the company, which later was to build in many parts of the Harrow area.

57. Paines Lane retains even to the present day many of its trees and hedges. This picture shows some of the early suburban houses carefully sited to retain the rural surroundings, something that later housing estates failed to achieve.

58. Cannon Lane was developed soon after the extension of the Metropolitan Railway from Harrow in 1885. City businessmen were urged to come and live at Pinner: *The neighbourhood abounds in picturesque scenery and many most delightful excursions can be made.*

PINNER — WAXWELL.

59. Waxwell Lane with the 'Wax Well' by the tree in the middle distance. The well was once one of the chief sources of water supply for Pinner.

Pinner Green, Pinner

60. Tranquility at the cross roads, Pinner Green. The blacked out street lamp dates this picture from the First World War. The road to the left leads to Pinner, whilst ahead the highway leads to Northwood.

Station Road, Pinner

61. Station Road, now Uxbridge Road. The station on the London and North Western Railway was called Pinner for many years. But after the opening of the Metropolitan Railway to the village centre in 1885, the name was changed to 'Hatch End for Pinner'. The lodge house seen here was at the gates of Old Hall. The great house was demolished in 1956, but the lodge remains.

NORTH HARROW

62. North Harrow station opened in 1915 and this picture shows the booking hut as seen from the Baker Street platform in about 1926. In the background is the Headstone Hotel nearing completion. The station tobacco and sweet kiosk is rather unhygienically sited in front of the station toilets! The station was rebuilt in 1927/28.

63. Construction of the 'Western Arterial Road' which was later called patriotically 'Imperial Drive'. Within two years of this photograph, new roads, shops and a cinema had transformed the old hamlet of Hooking Green into the suburb of North Harrow.

64. Unsurfaced roads and heaps of mud greeted homeseekers as they stepped out of North Harrow station in the late 1920's. They were faced with a bewildering choice of houses for sale. *On both sides of the line attractive houses are being laid out, and with pleasant vistas, gardening would seem to be the usual hobby* — extract from a 1931 guide book.

RAYNERS LANE

65. There really was a farmer Rayner and he lived in this interesting old farmhouse
between Rayners Lane and Pinner. In the 1930's the tide of progress swept the farm
away, replacing it by bright and hygienic semi-detached houses.

66. Building the bridge over the new railway at the future site of Rayners Lane station in 1903. Temporary tracks diverge towards Harrow and, right, South Harrow. The line opened on 4th July 1904, but the station came later, in 1906.

67. When this picture was taken from Rayners Lane bridge, the contractors were still clearing up after building the Harrow and Uxbridge Railway.

68. Junction of the Metropolitan and District Railways in 1929. The houses of Harrow Garden Village were soon to rise on the land seen here, and the builder, E.S. Reid, paid for his own sidings to be laid down in order to bring materials for constructing the estate. The signal cabin was demolished by a run-away goods train in 1934.

69. Station bridge on 29th August 1929, when work had begun on Harrow Garden Village and the new highway to North Harrow. At that time the tiny halt was handling 20,000 passengers a year. By 1938, when the new station opened, the total was an amazing four million!

70. High summer 1930 along Rayners Lane. Behind the young lady, the last hay crop is being harvested. Soon afterwards, the meadows were covered with rows of houses, each with its 'labour saving' kitchen; stained glass window in the hallway, and a tiled bathroom upstairs.

71. E.S. Reid, a one time director of local highways for the Council, started his own building company and began work on the Metropolitan Railway Country Estates' Harrow Garden Village Estate in 1929. He advertised: *This beautifully laid out, well timbered estate of over 213 acres, with 16 acres of permanent open space, recreation grounds and tennis courts, adjacent to Rayners Lane station, is within 11 miles of Baker Street.*

72. Countryside in transition: the early 1930's were boom years for housing development at Harrow. This view shows Rayners Lane by the junction with The Ridgeway in 1930. The fields are full of estate agents boards, and new homes are already rising on the hill towards Pinner.

SOUTH HARROW

73. This man is the last of his kind — one of that 'race' of navvies who worked and drank their way across England as they built the canals and the railways of the nineteenth century. Notice the brick 'oven' for cooking poached rabbits. Also his ample belt and braces, and the traditional straps around the legs of his trousers. Photographed on the Harrow and Uxbridge Railway — Roxeth, 1903.

74. Christ Church, Roxeth, was consecrated in 1862. The Reverend John Floyd Andrewes was vicar from 1877 to 1907, and he was a distinctive figure, as he walked along the muddy roads of Roxeth dressed in old fashioned long cassock and a 'shovel' style of hat.

75. At work on the railway viaduct between Roxeth and Rayners Lane in 1903. Temporary railway track has been laid over the fields to bring up building materials, as there were few roads in the area at that time.

IN THE GROUNDS & SHELTER—
"PADDOCKS", STH HARROW.

76. Generations of children would come to spend the day of their lives at The Paddocks in Northolt Road. The proprietor, A.B. Champniss, advertised a variety of attractions, including a miniature steam railway, donkey rides, sports fields and accommodation for 3,000 visitors under cover if there was wet weather. The Paddocks land was eventually sold for housing, but part of the wooded land was incorporated into Alexandra Park.